MAGIC HANGUL COLLECTION

MY KOREAN ALPHABET

COLORING BOOK

THIS BOOK BELONGS TO:

Learn the Korean Consonants,
Shapes and Parts of the Body!

M

MIGHTYFORTRESS
PRESS

EMAIL US AT
info@mightyfortresspress.com
TO GET THE FREE VIDEO LESSONS FOR THIS BOOK!

Just title the email
"Korean Alphabet Coloring Book."

Find us on 🅕 🅞 ▶
@mightyfortresspress

ISBN NO: 978-1-7328644-1-2
Text and illustrations Copyright 2020 by Mighty Fortress Press.

For general information on our other products, please contact our Customer Care Department within the U.S. by going to our website at www.mightyfortresspress.com.

Kang, Eunice, author.
Koh, Young Jae, book designer.
"Magic Hangul Collection"

TABLE OF CONTENTS

NOTE TO PARENTS

Welcome to *My Korean Alphabet Coloring Book of Consonants!* As an educator and a parent, I made this book because I wanted to teach my children the basics of Korean with instructions in the English language. To get the most out of this book, please take your time going through each page together with your child and practice how to say the sounds and names for each letter and word.

The illustrations are paired with the words written in Korean and in English phonetically so that Korean as second language learners can pronounce the Korean words. And even though this book is primarily a coloring book for young children, it could also be used as flashcards for older kids and beginner adults.

This book is divided into 4 units:
- 14 basic consonants
- 14 simple Korean words that begin with each consonant
- 6 shapes
- 7 parts of the body

There is a plethora of research that suggests learning a second language can boost the brain! Learning a second language benefits not only children as they learn to speak but also adults as they age. I hope that you and your family will find this book useful with hours of fun, coloring, and lots of learning. Thank you again for choosing this book.

Happy coloring and learning!

-Eunice Kang, Ph.D.

UNIT 1

CONSONANTS

자음

[ja-eum]

Note: In this unit, we will learn the names and sounds of each of the 14 basic Korean consonants.

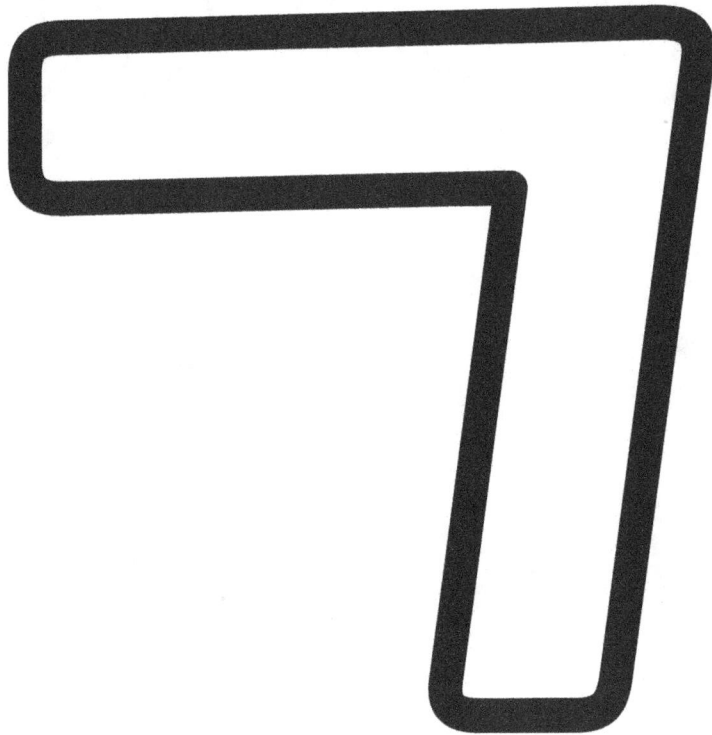

ㄱ

[gi-yuk]

The name of this consonant is [gi-yuk] and its sound is [g].

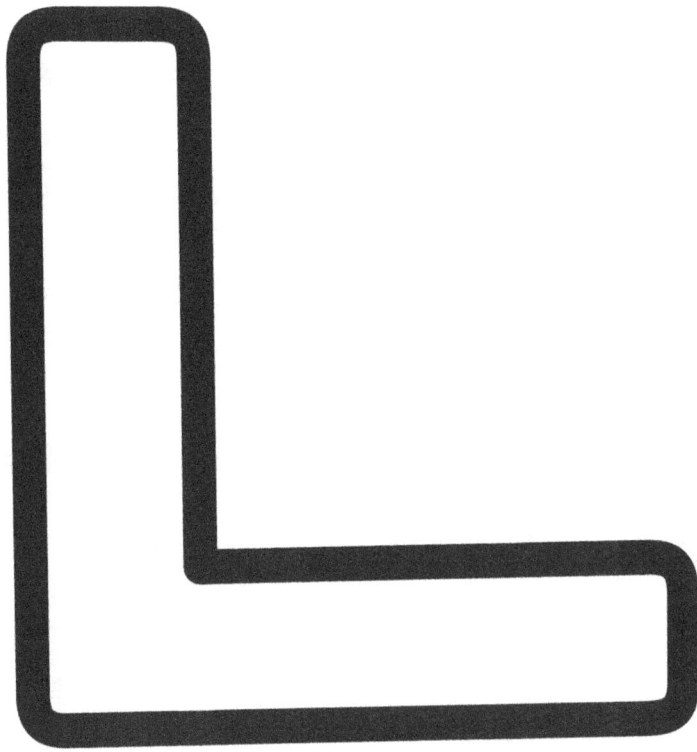

[nee-un]

The name of this consonant is [nee-un] and its sound is [n].

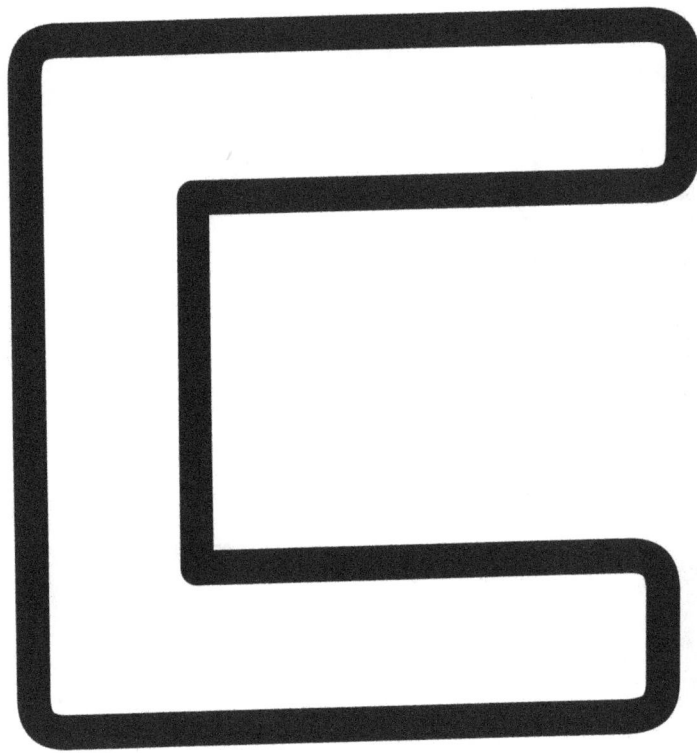

[dee-gut]

The name of this consonant is [dee-gut] and its sound is [d].

[ree-eul]

The name of this consonant is [ree-eul] and its sound is [r].

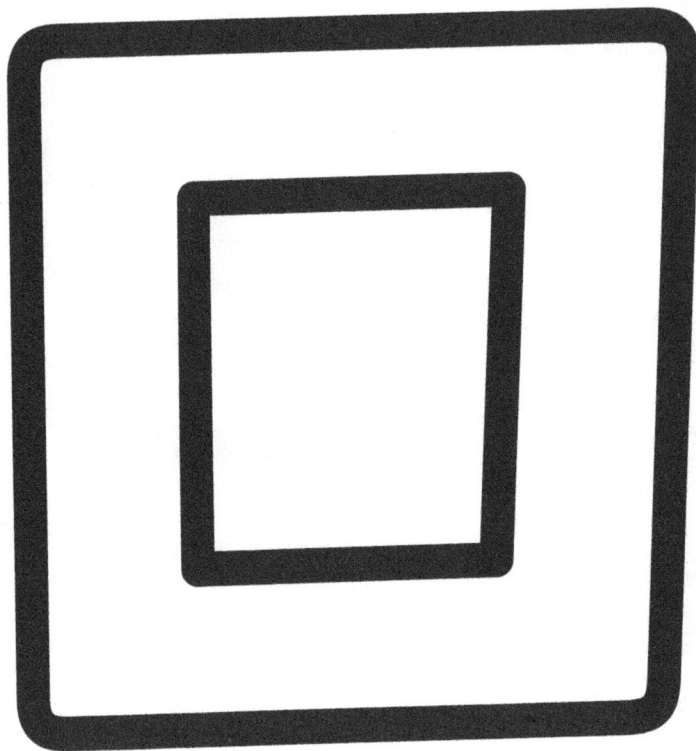

[mee-eum]

The name of this consonant is [mee-eum] and its sound is [m].

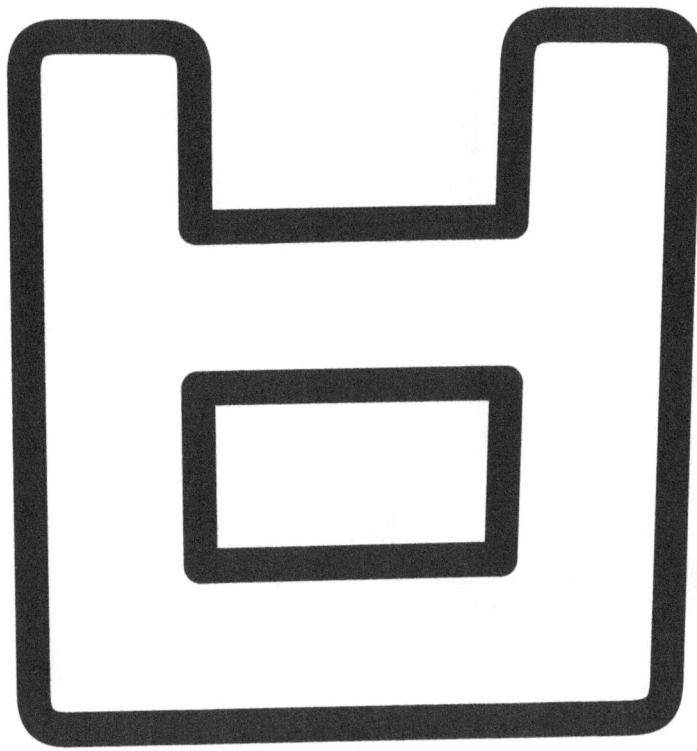

[bee-eup]

The name of this consonant is [bee-up] and its sound is [b].

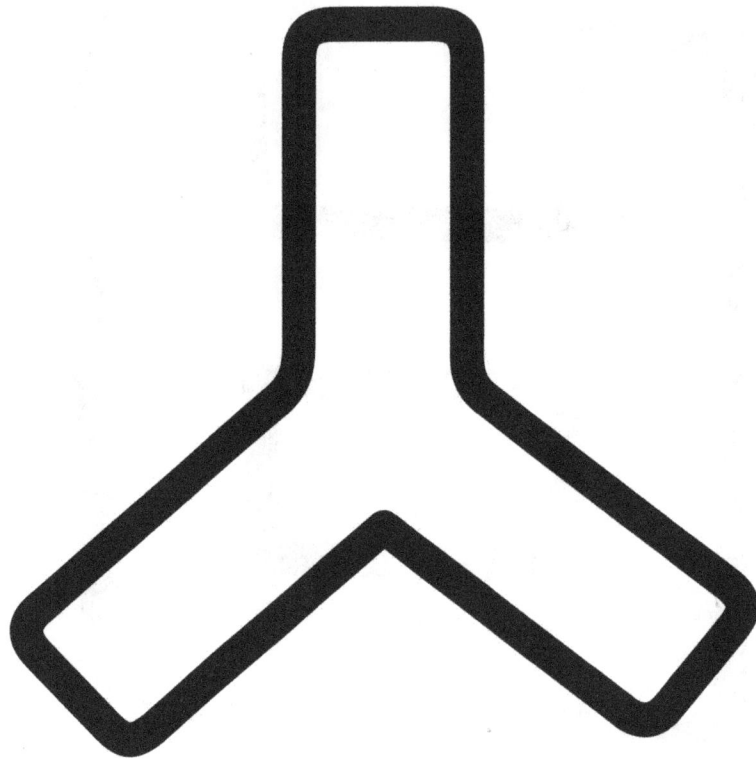

[shee-ot]

The name of this consonant is [shee-ot] and its sound is [s].

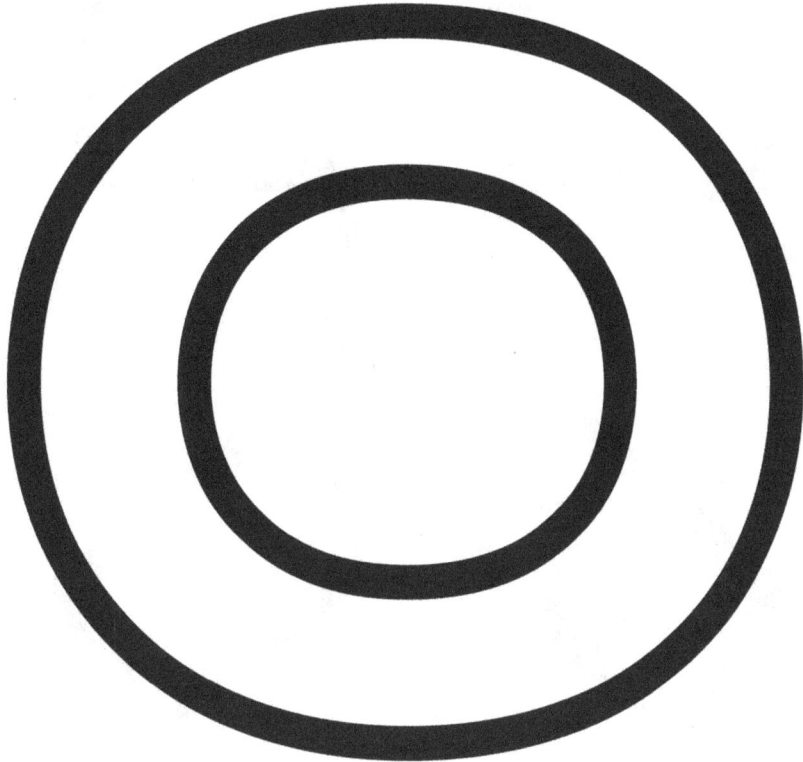

[ee-eung]

The name of this consonant is [ee-eung] and it has no sound.

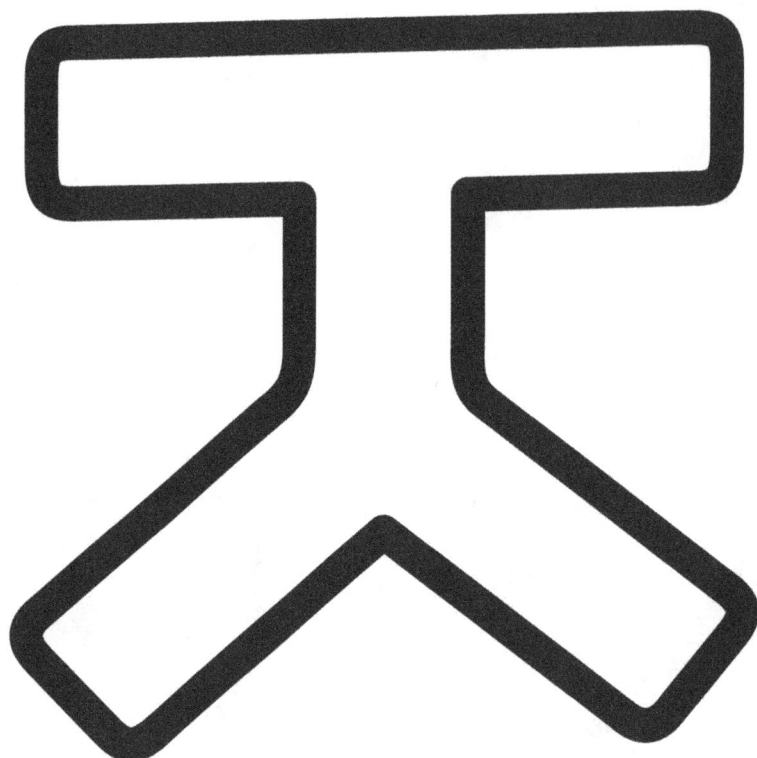

[jee-eut]

The name of this consonant is [jee-eut] and its sound is [j].

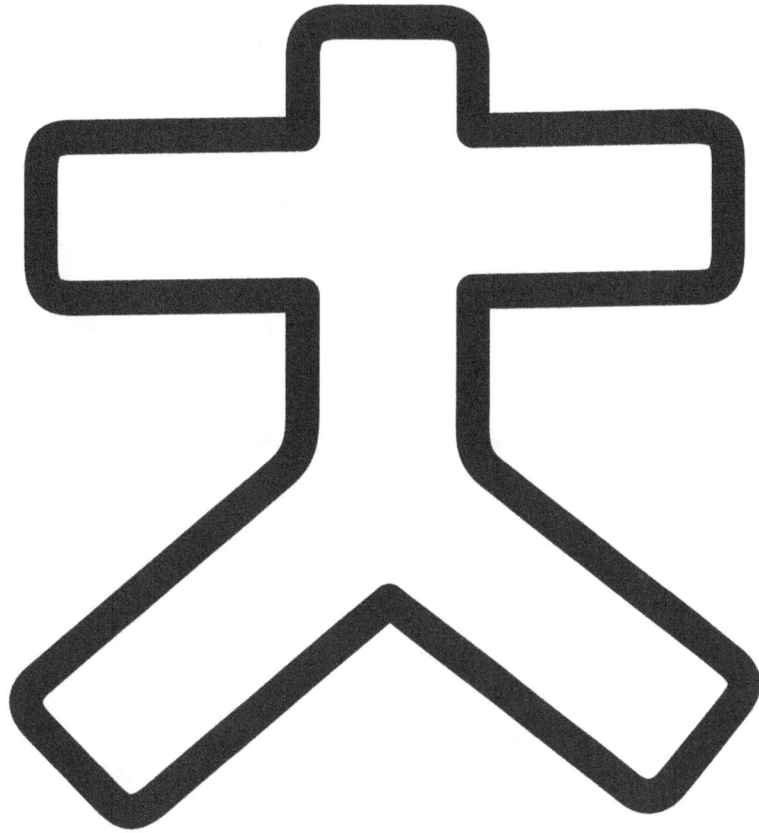

[chee-eut]

The name of this consonant is [chee-eut] and its sound is [ch].

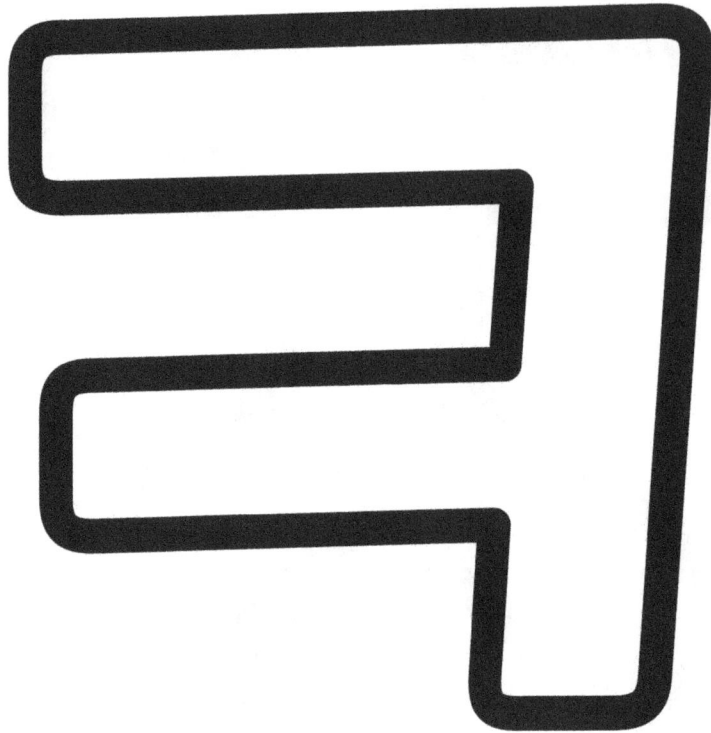

[kee-eut]

The name of this consonant is [kee-eut] and its sound is [k].

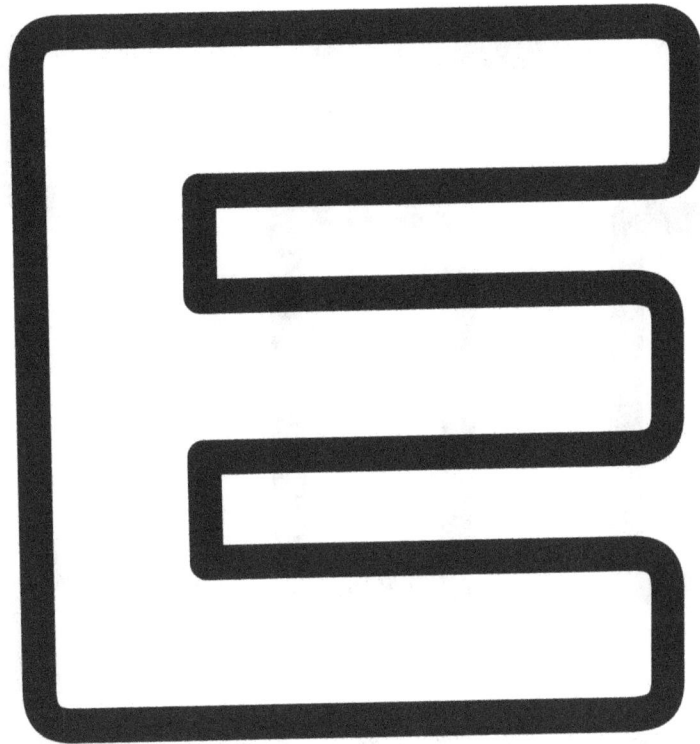

[tee-eut]

The name of this consonant is [tee-eut] and its sound is [t].

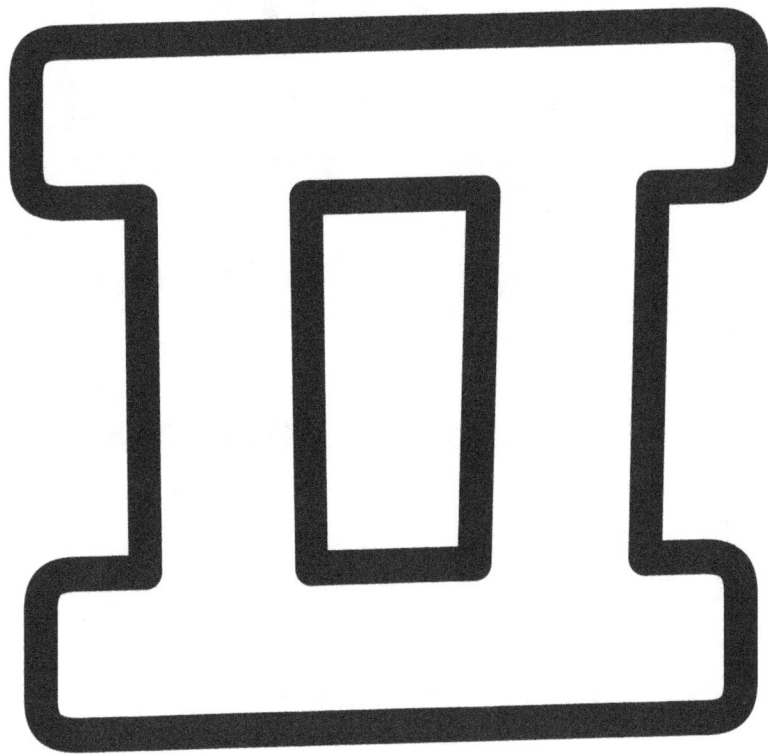

[pee-eup]

The name of this consonant is [pee-eup] and its sound is [p].

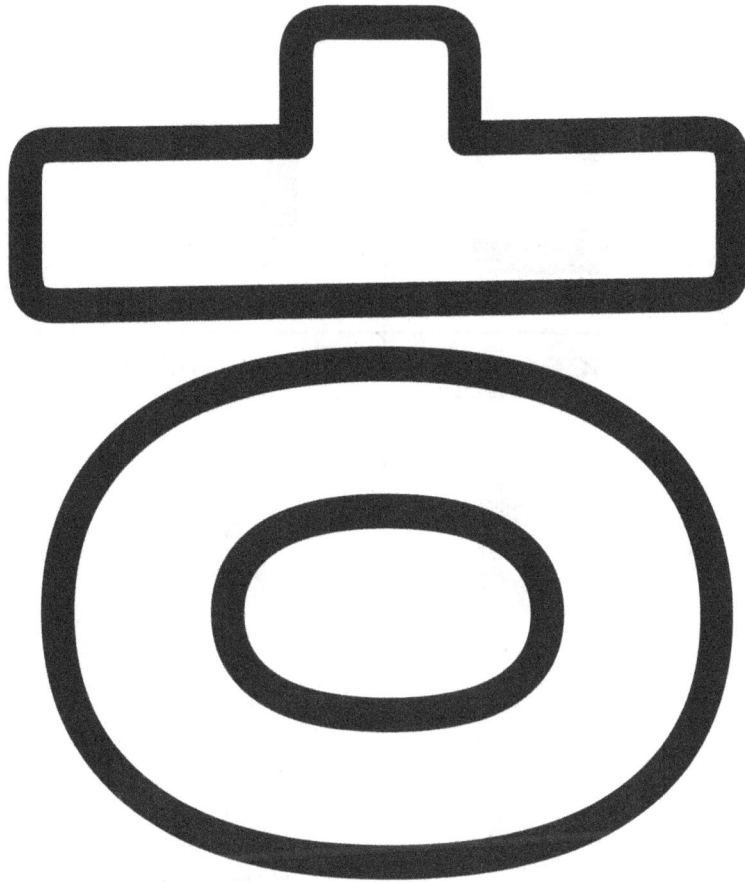

[hee-eut]

The name of this consonant is [hee-eut] and its sound is [h].

Recap of Unit 1
Consonants
자음 [ja-eum]

ㄱ	ㄴ	ㄷ	ㄹ
[gi-yuk]	[nee-un]	[dee-gut]	[ree-eul]
ㅁ	ㅂ	ㅅ	ㅇ
[mee-eum]	[bee-eup]	[shee-ot]	[ee-eung]
ㅈ	ㅊ	ㅋ	ㅌ
[jee-eut]	[chee-eut]	[kee-eut]	[tee-eut]
		ㅍ	ㅎ
		[pee-eup]	[hee-eut]

UNIT 2

KOREAN WORDS

단어

[da-nuh]

Note: In this unit, we will learn 14 simple Korean words that begin with each consonant.

7 is for

기차

[gi-cha]

L is for

나비

[na-bee]

ㄷ is for

다람쥐
[da-ram-juee]

ㄹ is for

라면
[ra-myun]

 is for

모자

[mo-ja]

 is for

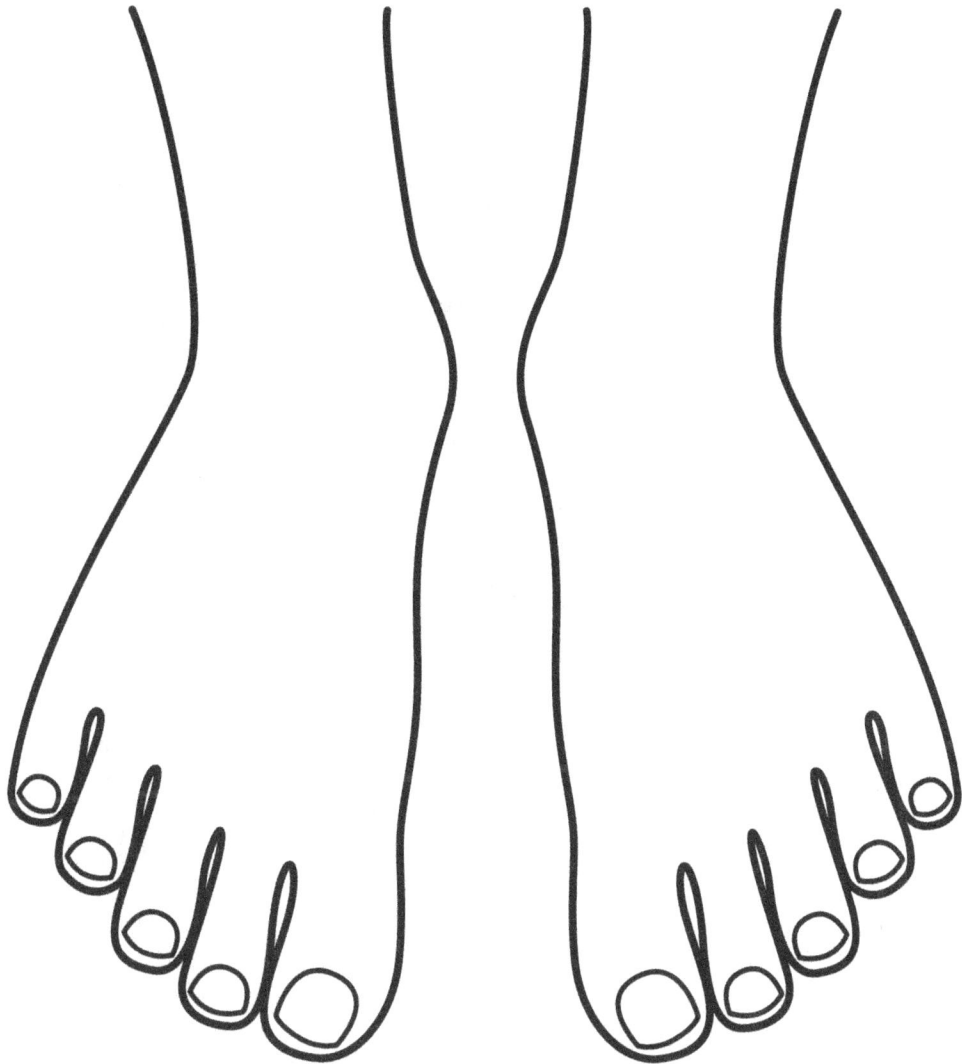

[bal]

 is for

사자

[sa-ja]

◎ is for

아기

[ah-gi]

ㅈ is for

자동차
[ja-dong-cha]

 is for

책상
[chaek-sahng]

ㅋ is for

케이크

[kae-ee-kuh]

E is for

태권도

[tae-kwon-do]

ㅍ is for

파인애플

[pa-in-ae-pull]

ㅎ is for

해

[hae]

Recap of Unit 2
Korean Vocabulary
단어 [da-nuh]

기차	나비	다람쥐	라면	모자
[gi-cha]	[na-bee]	[da-ram-juee]	[ra-myun]	[mo-ja]

발	사자	아기	자동차	책상
[bal]	[sa-ja]	[ah-gi]	[ja-dong-cha]	[chaek-sahng]

케이크	태권도	파인애플	해
[kae-ee-kuh]	[tae-kwon-do]	[pa-in-ae-pull]	[hae]

UNIT 3

SHAPES

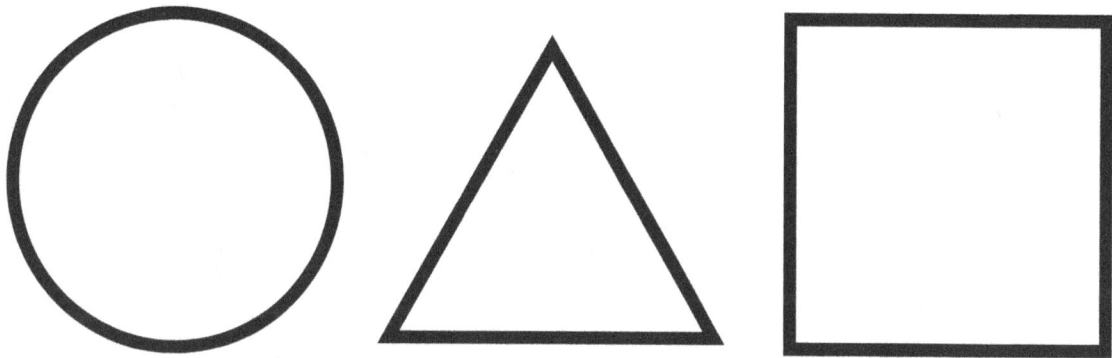

모양

[mo-yang]

Note: In this unit, we will learn 6 basic shapes.

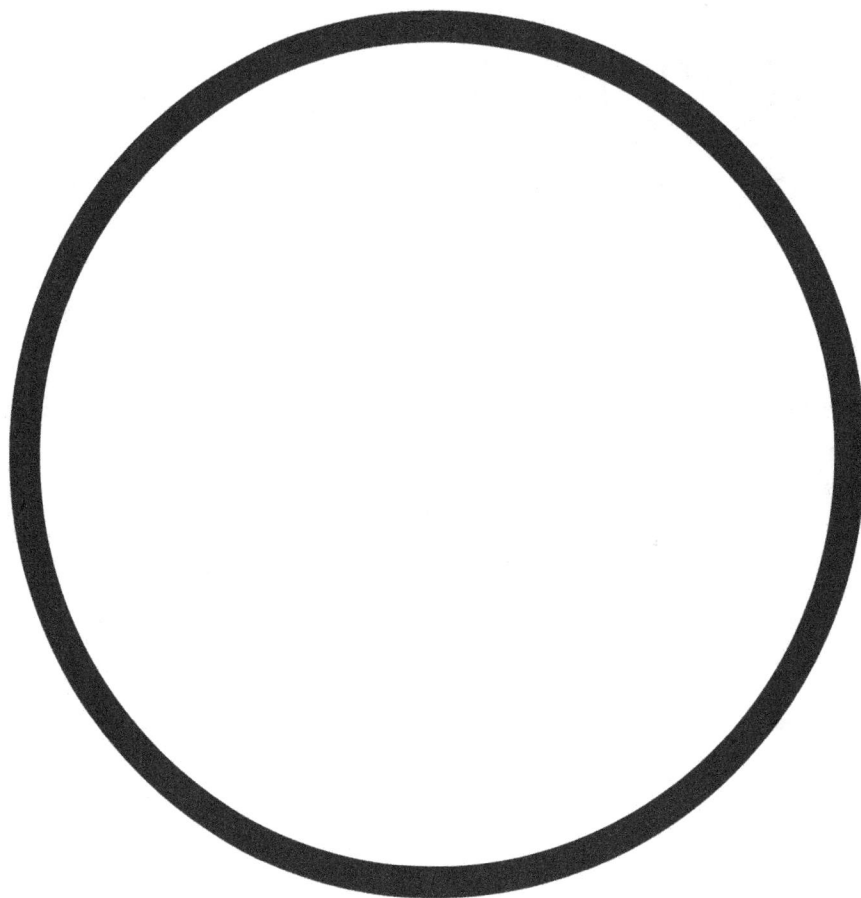

동그라미

[dong-gu-ra-me]

세모

[se-mo]

네모

[nae-mo]

직사각형

[jik-sa-gak-hyung]

하트

[ha-tuh]

별

[byul]

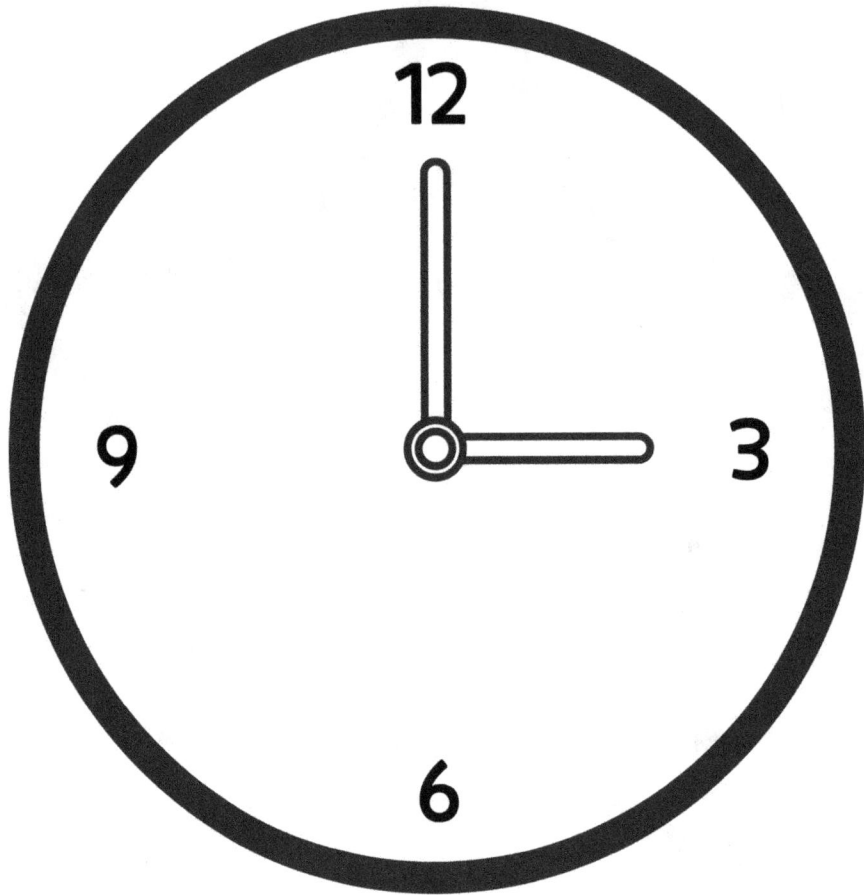

동그라미

[dong-gu-ra-me]

세모

[se-mo]

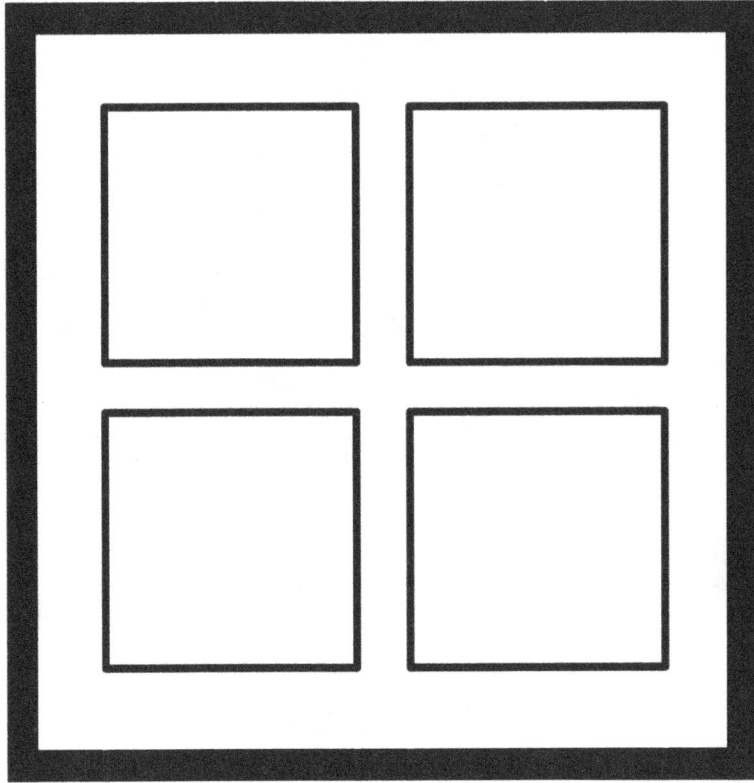

네모

[nae-mo]

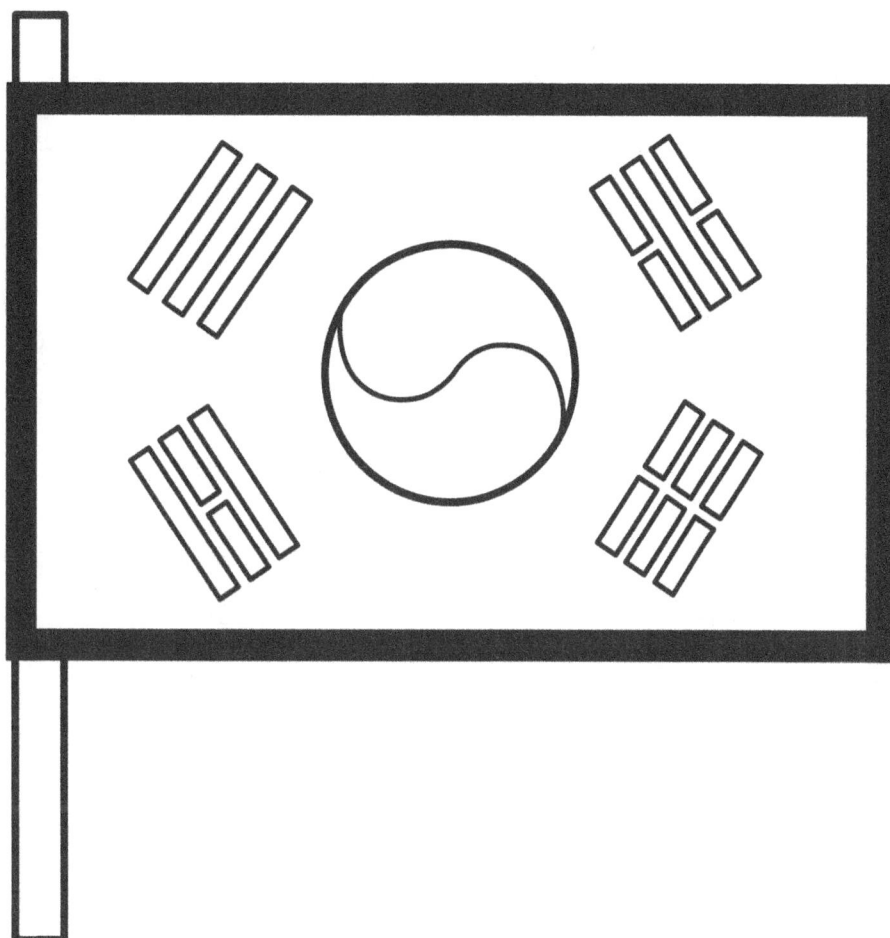

직사각형

[jeek-sa-gak-hyung]

하트

[ha-tuh]

별

[byul]

Recap of Unit 3
Shapes
모양 [mo-yang]

○	△	□
동그라미	**세모**	**네모**
[dong-gu-ra-mi]	[se-mo]	[nae-mo]

▭	♡	☆
직사각형	**하트**	**별**
[jik-sa-gak-hyung]	[ha-tuh]	[byul]

UNIT 4

PARTS OF THE BODY

몸

[mohm]

Note: In this unit, we will learn 7 different parts of the body.

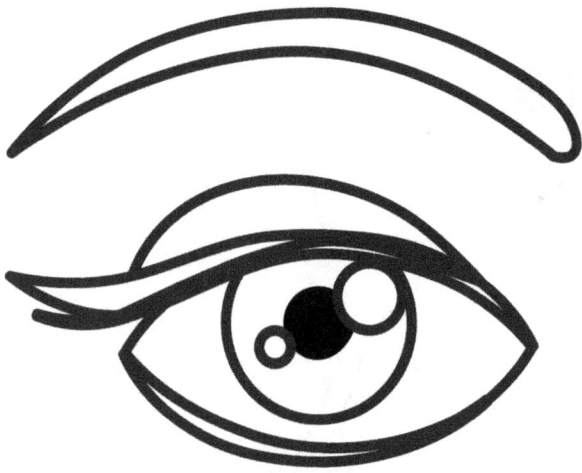

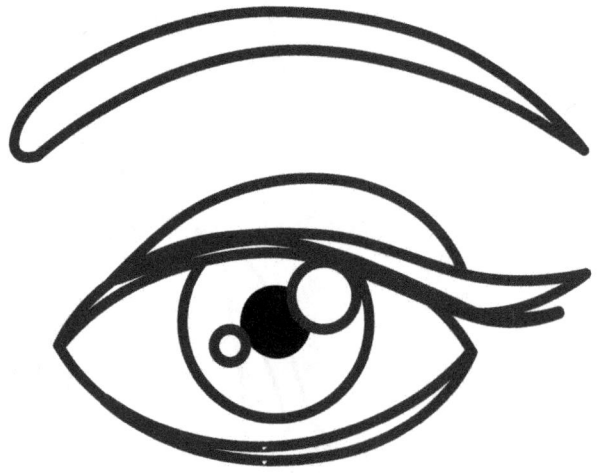

[noon]

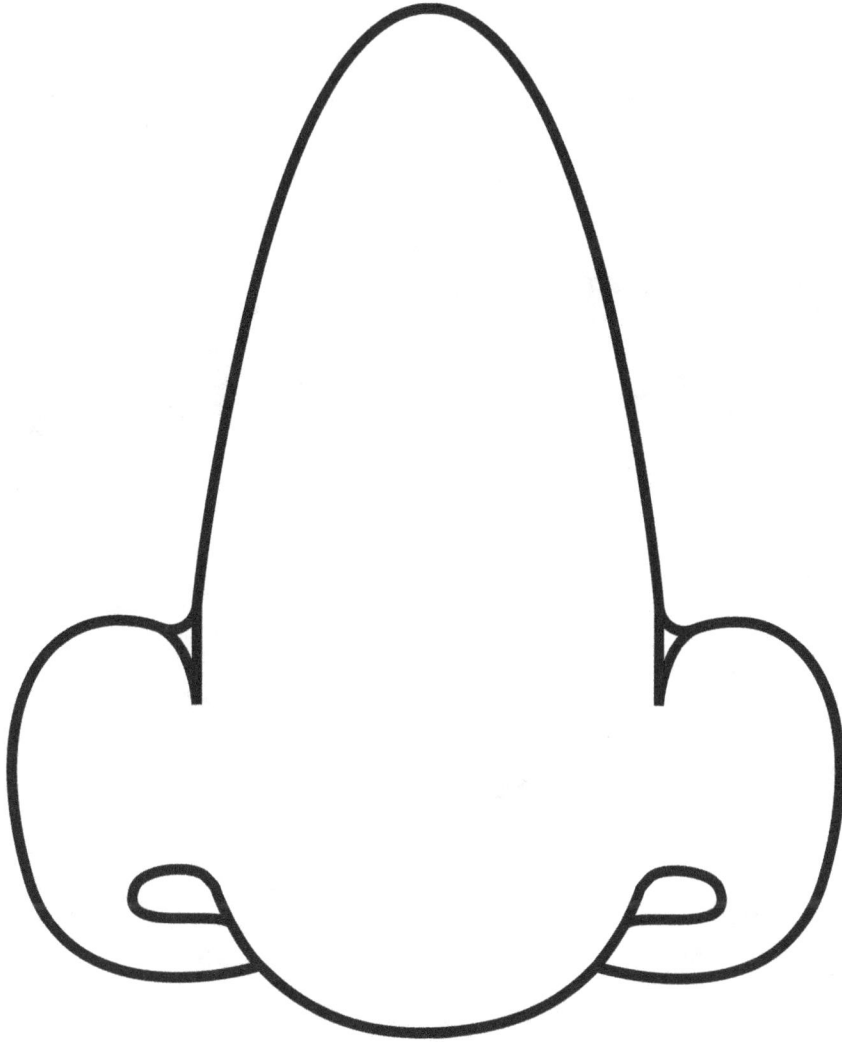

코

[koh]

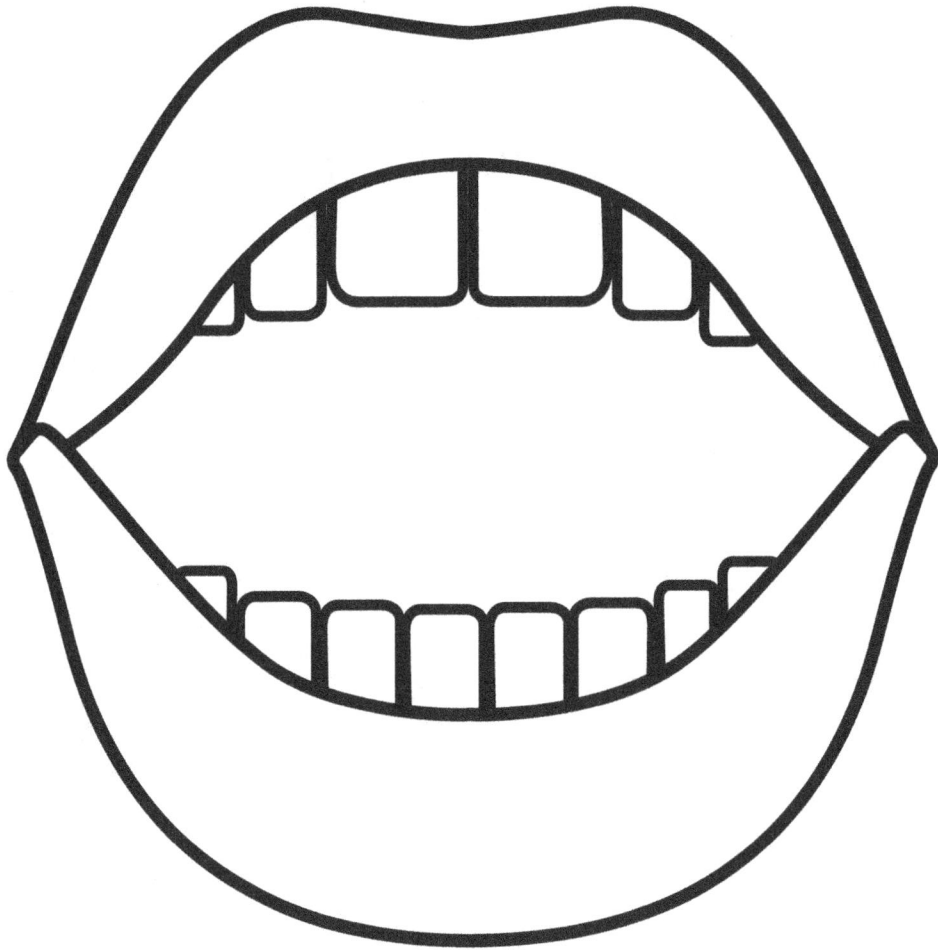

입

[eep]

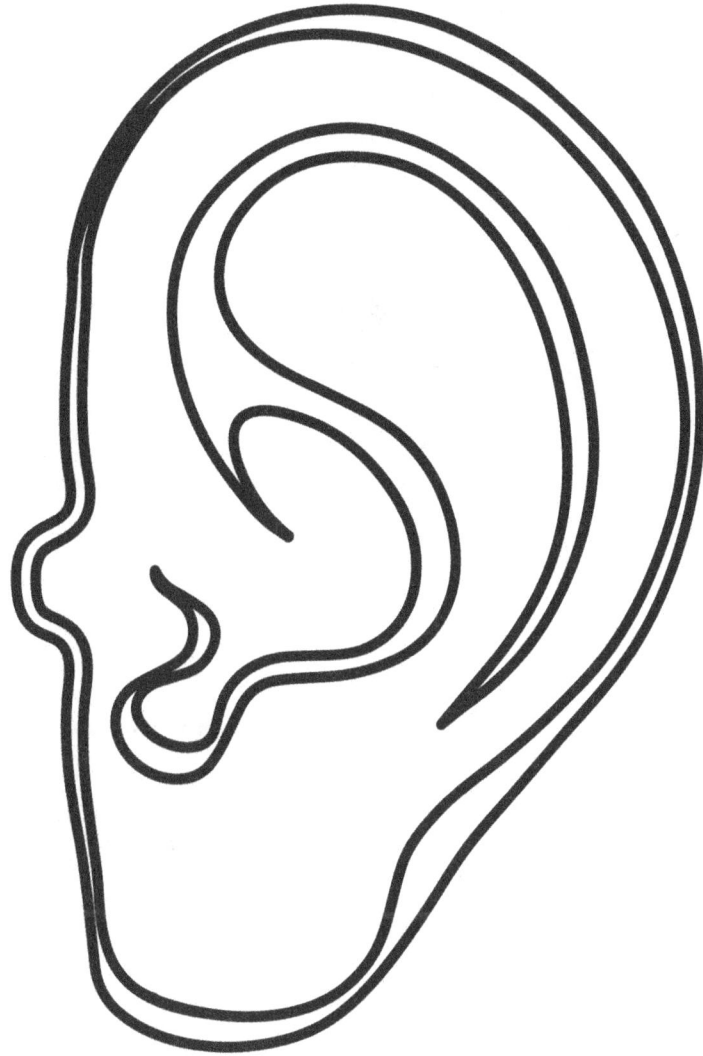

귀

[gyee]

손

[sohn]

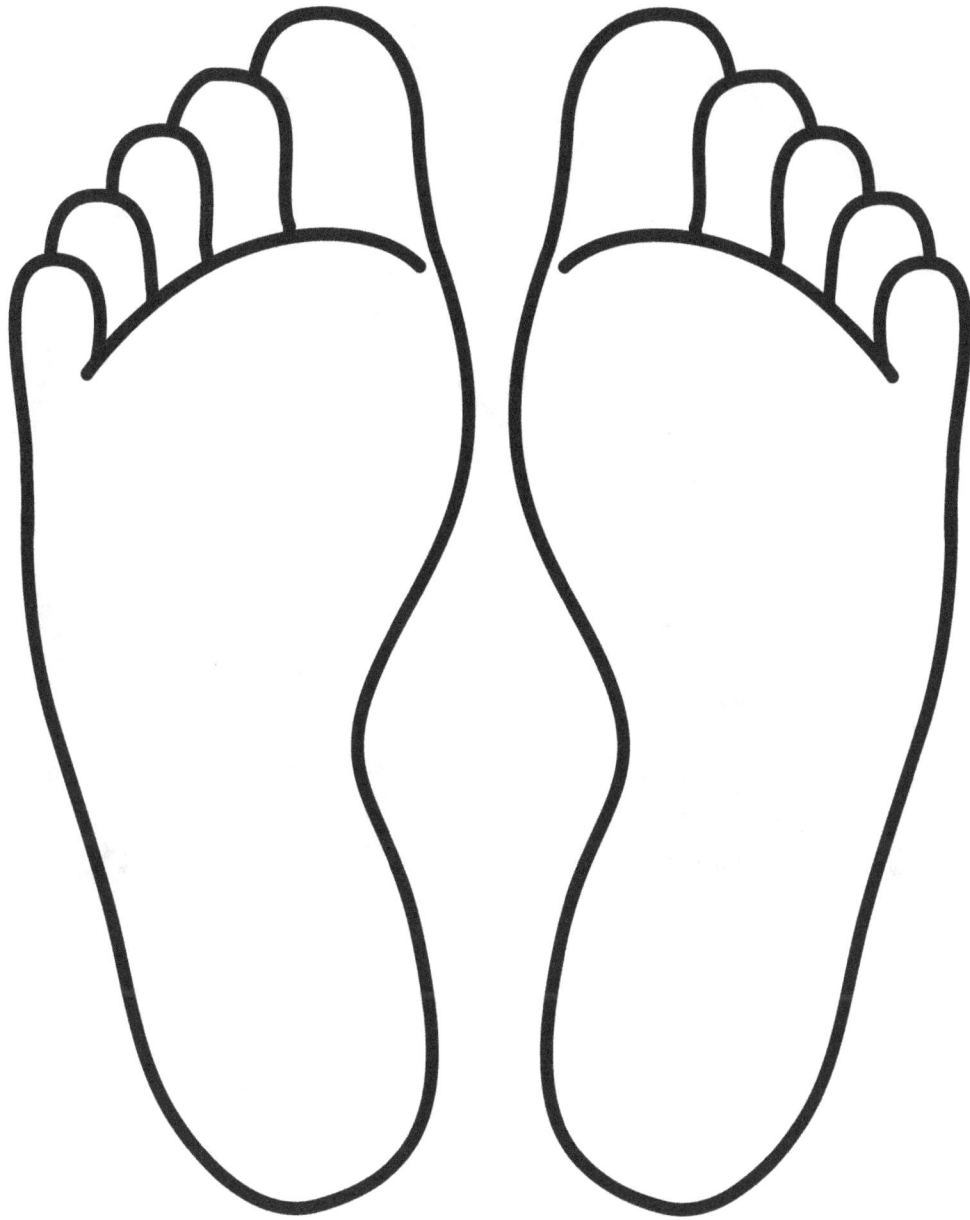

발

[bal]

머리

[muh-ree]

Recap of Unit 4
Body

몸 [mohm]

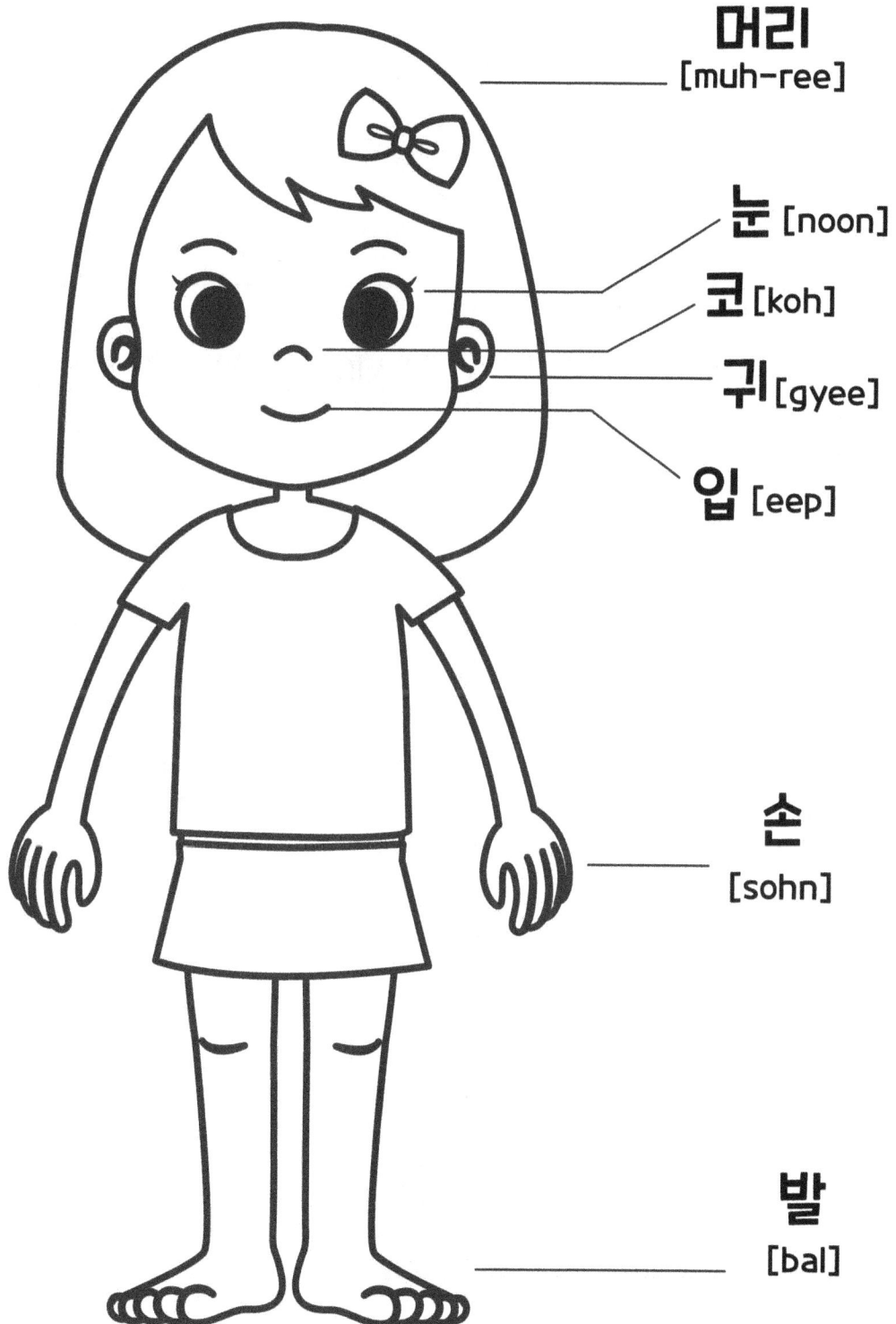

머리
[muh-ree]

눈 [noon]

코 [koh]

귀 [gyee]

입 [eep]

손
[sohn]

발
[bal]

Author

Eunice Kang, Ph.D. is an educator in Los Angeles, California. Her research areas include South Korea and Korean language policy. She loved coloring as a child and now loves coloring with her own two children.

f **◎** @eunicekangbooks

Book Designer

Young Jae Koh is a graphic designer based in Los Angeles, California. She has previously worked in Korea and New York as an art director. She loves to watercolor and create art with her daughter.

◎ @youngjaekoh

CHECK OUT MORE BOOKS BY MIGHTY FORTRESS PRESS!

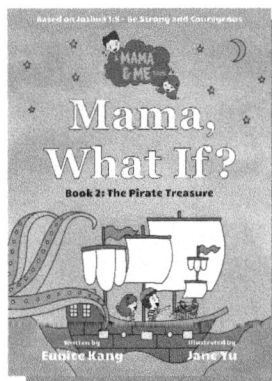

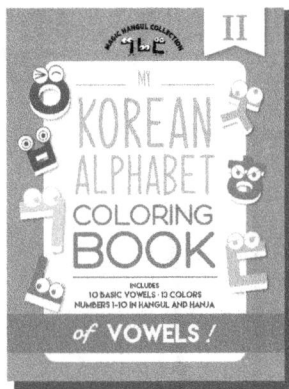

Korean
Writing Book

Coming
Soon.

www.ingramcontent.com/pod-product-compliance
Lightning Source LLC
Chambersburg PA
CBHW081227020426
42331CB00012B/3098